EXOTIC CATS

KATIE LAJINESS

Big Buddy Books
n Imprint of Abdo Publishing
abdopublishing.com

BIG BUDDY CATS

abdopublishing.com

Published by Abdo Publishing, a division of ABDO, PO Box 398166, Minneapolis, Minnesota 55439.

Big Buddy Books™ is a trademark and logo of Abdo Publishing.

Printed in the United States of America, North Mankato, Minnesota.
092017
012018

THIS BOOK CONTAINS RECYCLED MATERIALS

Cover Photo: Getty Images.
Interior Photos: Alamy Stock Photo (p. 19); Getty Images (pp. 5, 7, 9, 11, 13, 15, 17, 21, 23, 25, 27, 29, 30).

Coordinating Series Editor: Tamara L. Britton
Contributing Editor: Jill Roesler
Graphic Design: Jenny Christensen

Publisher's Cataloging-in-Publication Data

Names: Lajiness, Katie, author.
Title: Exotic cats / by Katie Lajiness.
Description: Minneapolis, Minnesota : Abdo Publishing, 2018. | Series: Big buddy cats | Includes online resources and index.
Identifiers: LCCN 2017943921 | ISBN 9781532111983 (lib.bdg.) | ISBN 9781614799054 (ebook)
Subjects: LCSH: Exotic shorthair cat--Juvenile literature. | Cats--Juvenile literature
Classification: DDC 636.82--dc23
LC record available at https://lccn.loc.gov/2017943921

CONTENTS

A POPULAR BREED

Cats are popular pets. About 35 percent of US households have a cat. And, Americans own more than 85 million!

Around the world, there are more than 40 **domestic cat breeds**. One of these is the exotic cat. Let's learn why the exotic is the most popular cat breed in the United States.

Garfield, the cartoon cat, was created to look like an exotic.

THE CAT FAMILY

All cats belong to the **Felidae** family. There are 37 **species** in this family. **Domestic cats** are part of one species. Lions and other types of cats make up the others.

Did you know?

Humans and cats have lived together for at least 3,500 years.

Domestic cats do not require a lot of space. They do well in small apartments or houses.

EXOTIC CATS

The exotic cat **breed** began in the 1950s. **Breeders** wanted a short-haired cat that looked and acted like a Persian. So, they bred American shorthair cats with Persian, Burmese, and Russian blue cats.

Did you know?

Exotic cats were first called Sterling cats because of their coat color.

People sometimes call this breed the teddy bear cat.

Although they are similar to Persians, **breeders** wanted these new cats to stand out. In 1967, the **Cat Fanciers' Association** teamed up with an American shorthair supporter. They agreed to start a new **breed** called the exotic.

Exotic cats are more playful than Persians. They love playing with toys and balls of string.

WHAT THEY'RE LIKE

The exotic is a quiet and sweet cat. Known for its loving nature, the exotic enjoys being around people. And, this is a cat that likes to sleep in its owner's lap!

Exotics get along well with dogs, children, and other cats.

COAT AND COLOR

This **breed's** coat comes in any color and any pattern. With their thick coats, these cats look like short-haired Persians. Their coats are slightly longer than other shorthaired breeds.

The exotic has a double coat. Two layers of fur help keep the cat warm and dry.

SIZE

The exotic is a medium-sized **breed**. They grow up to seven to 12 pounds (3 to 5 kg). With short legs, exotic cats stand closer to the ground than other cats.

These cats have flat faces and full cheeks. They have small, wide-set ears and big eyes.

Exotic cats rarely use their claws.

FEEDING

Healthy cat food includes beef, chicken, or fish. A good name-brand food will provide the **nutrients** a cat needs.

Cat food can be dry, semimoist, or canned. Food labels will show how much and how often to feed a cat.

Many cats are attracted to water fountains. Running water may encourage them to drink more water.

CARE

Cats need regular care to keep them healthy. The exotic cat's smooth coat is simple to **groom**.

Every ten to 14 days, cats need their claws trimmed. A scratching post can help a cat keep its claws short.

An exotic is perfect for those who like Persian cats, but not daily grooming.

Exotic cats need a good veterinarian. The vet can provide health exams and **vaccines**. He or she can also **spay** or **neuter** cats.

Kittens need to see the vet several times during their first few months. Adult cats should visit the vet once a year for a checkup.

Some exotic cats have trouble breathing because of their short noses.

Cats have an **instinct** to bury their waste. So, cats should use a **litter box**. Waste should be removed from the box daily.

A cat buries its waste to mark its area. If a cat goes outdoors, it will begin to do the same. A **microchip** can help bring a cat home if it gets lost.

Regularly clean an exotic cat's eyes. Tear ducts overflow leaving stains on its facial fur.

KITTENS

An exotic cat mother is **pregnant** for 63 to 65 days. Then, she gives birth to a **litter** of about five kittens. For the first two weeks, kittens mostly eat and sleep.

All kittens are born blind and deaf. After two weeks, they can see and hear. At three weeks, kittens begin taking their first steps.

Kittens are born without any teeth. Later, they will grow 30 adult teeth.

THINGS THEY NEED

Between 12 and 16 weeks old, exotic kittens are ready for **adoption**. Kittens like to be active. So, they need daily exercise. An exotic cat will be a loving companion for about 15 years.

Cats sleep more as they age. Many older cats sleep up to 20 hours a day.

GLOSSARY

adoption the process of taking responsibility for a pet.

breed a group of animals sharing the same appearance and features. To breed is to produce animals by mating.

breeder someone who breeds animals.

Cat Fanciers' Association established in 1906, it is the world's largest registry for pedigreed cats.

domestic cats tame cats that make great pets.

Felidae the scientific Latin name for the cat family. Members of this family are called felines. They include domestic cats, lions, tigers, lynx, and cheetahs.

groom to clean and care for.

instinct a way of behaving, thinking, or feeling that is not learned, but natural.

litter all of the kittens born at one time to a mother cat.

litter box a place for house cats to leave their waste.

microchip an electronic circuit placed under an animal's skin. A microchip contains identifying information that can be read by a scanner.

neuter (NOO-tuhr) to remove a male animal's reproductive glands.

nutrient (NOO-tree-uhnt) something found in food that living beings take in to live and grow.

pregnant having one or more babies growing within the body.

spay to remove a female animal's reproductive organs.

species (SPEE-sheez) living things that are very much alike.

vaccine (vak-SEEN) a shot given to prevent illness or disease.

ONLINE RESOURCES

Booklinks
NONFICTION NETWORK
FREE! ONLINE NONFICTION RESOURCES

To learn more about exotic cats, visit **abdobooklinks.com**. These links are routinely monitored and updated to provide the most current information available.

INDEX